Sitecore is a registered trademark of Sitecore Corporation A/S, used by permission.

ISBN: 978-1-9997740-2-8

Design by Graeme Forrest

www.stylographicdesign.co.uk

Foreword

I like to think I have an eye for spotting and nurturing talent, and ideally Neil Shack would be on my list - however the credit for his rise to the Sitecore Summit is simply down to himself. Through genuine hard work and an endless quest to learn and push the boundaries, Neil has become one of the top experts in the Sitecore community (note to all Sitecore MVP wannabes... That is how you do it!). For Neil, bottling up this wealth of knowledge for self preservation isn't the game though. Like his efforts in life, he gives back and with "The little book of Sitecore tips" volume 1 and now volume 2, and we're the beneficiaries of his knowledge. Not only is this a good read, you seriously can't put it down! It's a book where you can instantly gain insight, and then act. While you learn, your client/organisation benefits... Win/Win! If you're reading the preview of this book, I'll save you time, stop and buy it now. In fact buy several copies! - *Dominic Hurst, MVP*

Acknowledgements

To those that made this possible:

Michael West, Matthew Dresser, Tamas Varga, Thomas Eldblom, Dominic Hurst, Deborah Lamb, my Dad, my Heavenly Father... The usual thank yous - you all know the drill by now!

Volume 2: the continuation of a never ending journey...

About The Author

 **Neil Shack** wrote volume one of The Little Book Of Sitecore Tips! He also created the Helix Base GitHub project, is a two-time Sitecore Symposium speaker, a community hackathon judge in 2018, and a Sitecore Technology MVP in both 2017 & 2018.

@nshack31

linkedin.com/in/neil-shack/

nshackblog.wordpress.com

github.com/muso31

Technical Reviewers

Michael West @MichaelWest101

Michael is a four-time Sitecore Technology MVP (2015-2018) and received the award in recognition of his active contribution to the Sitecore community including Sitecore Slack Chat and Sitecore Stack Exchange. He is a key contributor to the popular open source module Sitecore PowerShell Extensions (SPE), and advocate for the popular Sitecore Experience Accelerator (SXA).

Matthew Dresser @m_dresser

Matt has a passion for learning and knowledge sharing, often presenting at Sitecore user groups. He is a tech lead at Valtech and has been a Sitecore Technology MVP since 2016.

About This Book

Volume 2 has arrived! We all know sequels are never as good (unless it's a Godfather movie) but don't judge too harshly. Like the last book, this book is a light-hearted look at some useful Sitecore tips (current version is 9.0 rev. 171219 Update-1).

These tips are targeted at all levels of user but whether you're recapping or learning, I hope you find the book useful.

Do Your Research

Read **The Little Book Of Sitecore Tips Volume 1**! Honestly, who jumps straight in at the second part? And I don't care if you watched Star Wars IV, V and VI before Episode I.

Soooooooooooo Retro

Sometimes you end up attempting a difficult **retrofit** because you didn't plan ahead.

Retrofitting a Helix architecture for example, or refactoring fields from your template to make use of inheritance (causing data loss - see page 113). Why make work for yourself? Always try and *plan ahead.*

Serialize All The Things

Use **Unicorn**. It includes a **PowerShell** script to help with item serialization in your **CI/CD** pipeline. It even includes SPE commands to serialize content! It's neat; it works; it's well supported; it's configurable: it's a thumbs up in my book (literally!).

Think about your serialization strategy as soon as possible before adding content. The **new item evaluator** adds missing content and skips pre-existing items (aka *'deploy once'*); rest assured you won't lose any work. The **master evaluator** overwrites content every time. In the last tip we mentioned planning ahead, this also applies to your **Unicorn** serialization strategy. Everything benefits from forward planning.

301 Redirects

They're not available out of the box (but do come with SXA), so write yourself a processor in the **httpRequestBegin** pipeline and add a pile of **redirects** to the content tree (if you're not using IIS redirects). These can also be a very helpful option in an **Azure PaaS** instance.

It's time for that shameless plug again! Checkout the 301 redirect feature in **Helix Base**:

http://bit.ly/2B2YA35

#ReturnOfTheShamelessPlug

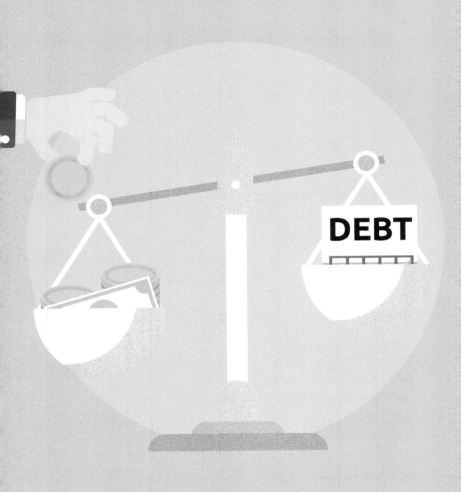

Pay Your Debts

It's a killer for all... **Technical debt**. Pay it off! Follow the '*boy scout principle*' and clean up as you go along - Like a thief in the night **tech debt** will creep up on you. Prevent it, and cure it where you can. Do not end up at the point of "Let's start again" or waste time spinning plates because you didn't setup a quality platform.

Far too many implementations are often riddled with technical debt. Don't rush to meet 'deadlines'. Make sure your staff know the Sitecore platform to an expert level. Sadly, the required skill-set is difficult to find... so read books and teach yourself! :wink:

...also upgrade your Sitecore instances, the **Express Migration Tool** exists for a very good reason!

Check The Database

Confused as to why something isn't appearing on the published site though it's present in the **Content Editor**? Don't forget to view your '**web**' database and see if the item is there. Great for debugging.

Unicorn Sync'age

Unicorn has an option to update your **search index** (and the link database) during a sync: use it.

Also, while we're on the **Unicorn** topic again; apply rule-based configuration (thank you Sitecore 9.x!) to ensure that **Unicorn** doesn't execute in CD environments and to change the *physicalRootPath* per environment. Remember to sync your **users** and **roles** too; If you're doing this, remember you have *removeOrphans="false"* at your disposal.

Transform Files... Or Not!

They used to be a lot more useful, but when it comes to deployments remember we now have **rule-based configuration**. Since you read the last tip you now know at least one example of where it can be used! Gone are the days of worrying about swapping configs, or tokenizing variables in your deployment pipelines.

When making use of **rule-based config** remember to configure a *role* (Standalone, ContentManagement etc) and a *localenv* (UAT, PreProd etc) in your web.config.

```
<add key="role:define" value="ContentManagement"/>
<add key="localenv:define" value="PreProd"/>
```

http://www.coretecdigital.com

Sync Your Environments

Often we need to keep our environments in **sync**, and there are plenty of ways to do this. Learn them all! Check out useful tools such as **RAZL, Sitecore Sidekick** and **Coast** for Sitecore. I like the Sidekick content migrator a lot.

And if it's only the **Web database** you need to replicate then the most simple and most native option is to use a **publish target**. When you're publishing files on a production environment why not have it deploy its content to another box? This can be particularly handy with the likes of an Azure PaaS setup when we want a database replicated across multiple regions.

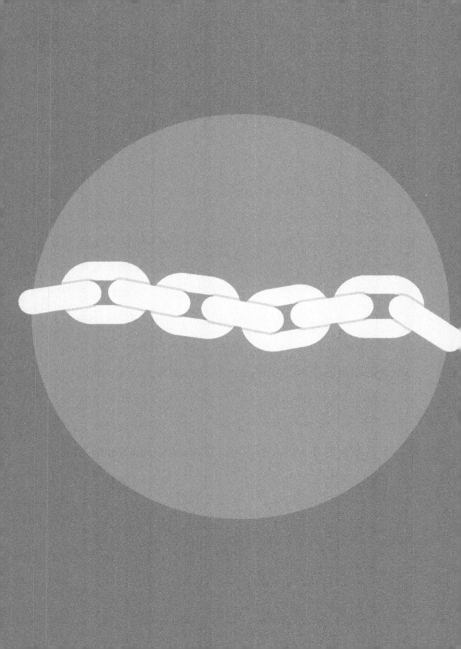

Link It Up

You can find a **link database** in your SQL core database. Make sure you're aware of this option and know how to use it. For example, write yourself an **admin tool** to show which items are based on a given template... Yes this example can be achieved by using the search tool found in the **Content Editor** but practice makes perfect, ok?

Here's a nice read **http://bit.ly/2rCY308**

Analytics'age

Wondering why your **Experience Analytics** are not being updated? Firstly, methods such as **SaveAndReleaseContactToXdb** are great for a localhost. Secondly, understand the **session end**, read the following:

http://bit.ly/2k5OWCc

Tidy That Tree!

Sometimes things look messy in the **Content Editor**. For example, you may have a **branch template** with a child **Components** folder to store your data source items, aka a 'local datasource'.

Use the '**hide**' option on this **Components** folder to present a more user-friendly experience. Items will still be visible in the **Experience Editor**, so do not fear.

Select the '**Configure**' tab, then '**Hide**'.

Where Am I?!

If you're making use of **Geo IP** be sure to create a handy admin tool:

http://bit.ly/2rLvGy6

Also read the Sitecore docs as it's important to gain an understanding of what is available to us in the **Geolocation Service** that will enable us to identify a user:

http://bit.ly/2GafJWo

JSON Data Model

We all work with Jason, what a guy! So get to know the **JSON data model** if you're having fun with the **Sitecore Experience Accelerator**:

http://bit.ly/2rbWcSX

If you're not having fun the SXA way then read all about **JSS** or....

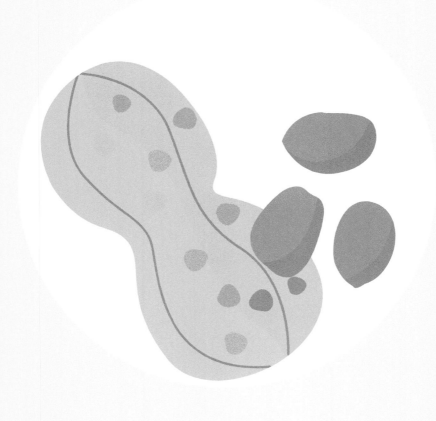

Sitecore Services In A Nutshell

...use Sitecore services:

In Sitecore 9 and earlier we have an **Item Service** to access Sitecore items, and an **Entity Service** to access business objects, both of which are **REST**ful **API's**. For example, we can get items using a **GET Request** with the **Item Service**:

http://YourInstance/sitecore/api/ssc/item/Some_Guid/children?fields=
ItemId,ItemName,TemplateName

In Sitecore 9 we now have the **OData Item Service**. Take a look at the following:

http://bit.ly/2DaJ3PT

Editable Rendering Parameters

Trying to make your **rendering parameters** editable fields in the **Experience Editor**? Stop right there! This is unsupported. Incidentally, if you're trying the same using **Glass** you'll receive an error message. I'm afraid it's **'Edit component properties'** for you.

Check Your License

Wanna see info about the **License** at the login screen? Here you go:

<setting name="Login.DisableLicenseInfo" value="false" />

Next time you visit the login screen you'll see a nice little '**License options**' link with some lovely license info. Don't forget that admin password now!

Credit for this one goes here **http://bit.ly/2IwpPpV**

Source Control No

Some files do not belong in **source control**, use patch files whenever possible. Folders such as **_node_modules_** and **_packages_** should not appear in **source control** either – sort those **_tf/gitignore_** files people!

Think about which Sitecore items actually belong in **source control**. Earlier we mentioned Unicorn, don't clog up your code base by serializing items that are not required.

http://www.coretecdigital.com

'Bare' Roots In Mind

Don't add settings to your **root item** - they should be added to the content tree as a separate item underneath. Why? Well in a multi-site setup we may use a query in the Datasource Location for the rendering; this will refer to the Template Id of the **root item** - but not every site will require the same settings, so these should be configured on a per site basis, and not on your **root item**.

⊿ ◉ Helixbase

▶ 🏠 Home

▶ ⚙ Settings

▶ 📁 Global

▶ 🖼 Media Library

'Bucketable' Your New Vocab Favourite

More than 100 items in a branch? Use a **bucket**.

#ShortestTipEver

...ok let's make this a bit more informative: you can also select '**Lock child relationship**' if you wish to ensure a **child item** always resides under a **parent item** in a **bucket**. You can find this option on the **Standard Values** of the parent template item in the 'Item Buckets' section.

Constructor Injection > Setter Injection

Injecting our dependencies in the constructor makes unit testing very easy to implement. **Constructor injection** means there is no hard coded dependency. While **setter injection** is useful for adding a default, it will almost never be required if we're using DI correctly. Stay away from poor man's DI and/or inheritance if you can inject a dependency in the constructor instead! I don't care if you think it doesn't need to be reusable, write reusable code regardless and make Uncle Bob proud. We'll need a practical knowledge of **SOLID** if we're taking the 'tech debt' tip on page 11 seriously.

...please also avoid the service locator anti pattern! #Filth

DependencyResolver.Current.GetService<IFilth>();

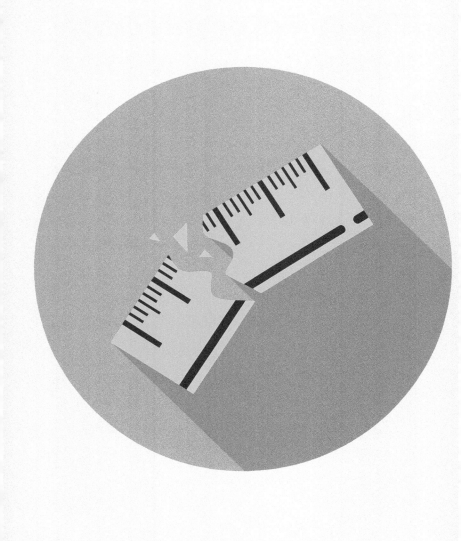

Rules Are Not There To Be Broken!

While Sitecore has a **'required'** rule, an admin user can still ignore it and publish an item. If that doesn't sit right, there is always an option to create a **compulsory field validation**. Add parameters to your field validation rule:

Result=FatalError

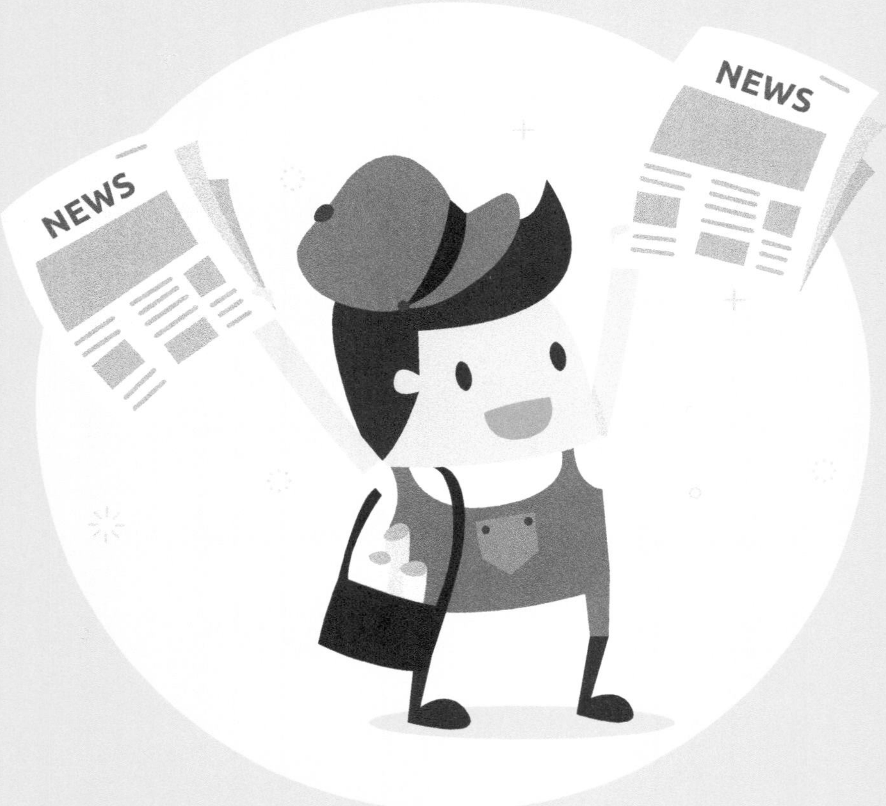
NEWS
NEWS

Publishing Power

Install the new **publishing service (SPS)**, as thanks to the likes of **SQL transactions**, it's lightening fast. It runs on a subset of **.NET Core** and allows us to easily debug, even as a console app.

There's a lot of work going on to decouple the Sitecore Kernel. The approach used on the publish service is an example of the way forward for the **Sitecore Framework** (not to be confused with SIF).

Sitecore Rocks!

It does, doesn't it? :heart: It's full of features that you should investigate. For example, did you know that **Sitecore rocks** has an auto publish? There you are working away on a view then *BAM...* it's in your webroot. Pretty neat. More on that later, but go and find out about as many **Sitecore rocks** features as you can as it will be time well spent.

Sitecore rocks is an example of how time spent investigating technology can be recuperated when we discover features that will save time in our daily activities. This applies to all technology, and it's a good way to prevent the **tech debt** that we already referred to. Brush up; do your homework: it'll pay in the long run. I don't want to hear "oh but I don't have time", the reason for that could very well be because you never spent time learning time saving methods.

Rap It Yo!

Wrap your API calls. For example, *Sitecore.Context.* should not appear throughout your code, or in pipeline processors - if it can be avoided.

Some things to **wrap**:

~~Glass API calls~~

~~Christmas presents~~

~~Tracker.Current.*~~

~~Language.Current.*~~

~~RenderingContext.Current.*~~

Knuckles

http://www.coretecdigital.com

Yummy Patterns

Yes you can use DI in pipelines, I wasn't lying earlier... **resolve="true"** when you register your processor - but still try and avoid the service locator anti pattern! #Filth

I've suggested writing reusable code with constructor injection - keep that going right throughout your code base, including your **pipelines**.

http://www.coretecdigital.com

Route In The Garbage

Content gone **missing**?! Everybody panicking? Wondering where on earth to get it from? Remember there's a **recycle bin...** I bet you it's sat there!

In the panic of missing content, this can be forgotten.

Helix Retro Headaches

If you retrofit a **Helix** architecture, you can often find that your references to **NuGet packages** will work locally, but as soon as it's on another machine... boom! Rather than becoming the token *"it works on my machine"* comedian, do this... open your **csproj** files in a text editor and add as many ..\ as you need to those paths for package references:

<HintPath>
..\..\..\..\packages\Glass.Mapper.Sc.Core.4.5.1.339-beta\lib
Mvc52\Glass.Mapper.Sc.Mvc.dll
</HintPath>

...but you read the **second tip** in this book and paid close attention, yes? Avoid the **retrofit**, nobody likes to hear "I told you so".

A Query On Queries

Remember that time when it was easy to test **Sitecore queries**? It's still there, honest, it's just hidden away now. After logging in, browse to:

/sitecore/shell/default.aspx?xmlcontrol=IDE

Then use **Tools->XPath Builder**

Or use:

http://url/sitecore/shell/default.aspx?xmlcontrol=IDE.XPath.Builder

It's A Goal!

He shoots, he scores! Did you know you can register a **goal** with a **query string**?

?sc_trk=[some_goal]

Great for client-side registrations.

Once Upon A Time In The West...

...you could **show field names** in the default placeholder text if the value was empty.

Not any more! Well, not totally true, we put that one right for all of you out there who appreciate a nice UX. You can now enable this on a per field basis: **http://bit.ly/2rEa5XX**

Or globally: **http://bit.ly/2B98DQg**

For me this has to be one of the **first things** you do when setting up a new instance of Sitecore.

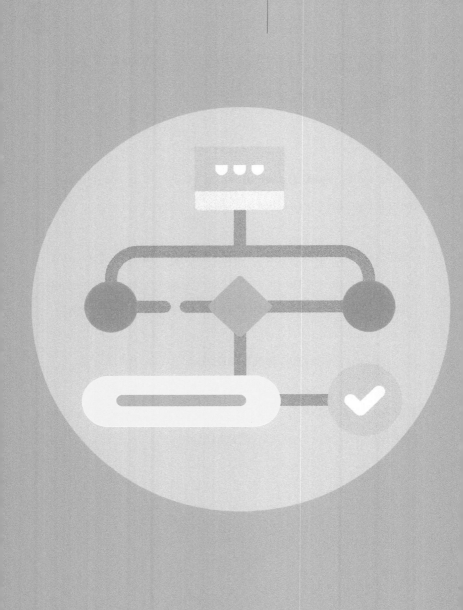

Work My Flow

When adding a workflow to standard values use the **'default workflow'** field and not the **'workflow'** one, **'workflow'** sounds right but you'll be adding a workflow to your standard values item - oops!

http://www.coretecdigital.com

Image Editor Fail'age

Working on a **multi lingual site** and trying to edit an image but see a lovely useless greyed out **Save** button?

Ensure the Role has **'language read'** and **'language write'** permissions to the **en** language as that's the context used for the button ¯_(ツ)_/¯

http://www.coretecdigital.com

No Insert Here

Picture the scene... your editor is working away and adds a new component, then they select a **current datasource** for their component and we're all happy with that, right?

Ok, scenario 2... now the editor comes back and adds a component but wants to insert a **new datasource**, but you decide that's crossing a line!

If you're a bit strict and want to prevent editors from adding **new datasource items** remove 'insert' from the custom experience buttons on the rendering, that ought to do the trick.

LAST PLACE

Last Patch Wins

There's a quick way to **patch** your processor at certain points in the pipeline. Below are examples of **last**, and **first**:

```
<processor patch:after="processor[type='*']"type="INFO_HERE" />


<processor patch:before="*[1]" type="INFO_HERE" />
```

http://www.coretecdigital.com

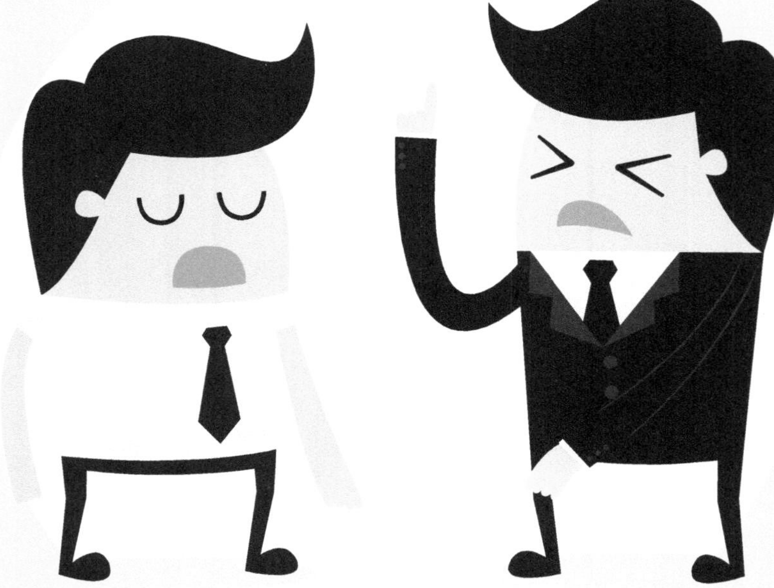

Dev No No's #2

Continuing the theme from **Volume 1**, more things not to say or write if you want to be taken seriously:

"Site-Core"

"We don't need components, I'll add HTML to the RTE"

"Ah Friday, great day for a launch wouldn't you say?"

"siteCore"

"It's ok we'll cherry pick everything"

...you have been warned! ...again! ...about some more things!

Having The Blues

Your users insert a **rendering**... they see a **blue dot**... you're a bad person! First go and scrub yourself in the shower...

...then come back and create a **thumbnail** for all of your **renderings**. With standard fields enabled you can see 'Thumbnail' under the 'Appearance' section. Add yourself a nice little **rendering thumbnail** for a better author experience. Feel free to add an Icon too.

Won't somebody please, think of the authors!

Lost Datasource Items

Can't see 'create new content' in your 'select the associated content' popup on your component? You didn't set a **Datasource Template** for the rendering.

This is great if you only want editors to be able to select **current datasource** items (which is also a useful tip) but for the most part we want authors to add new content for a component so if you're stuck, you now know what you forgot to do.

While we're on the topic of datasources... datasource all the things!

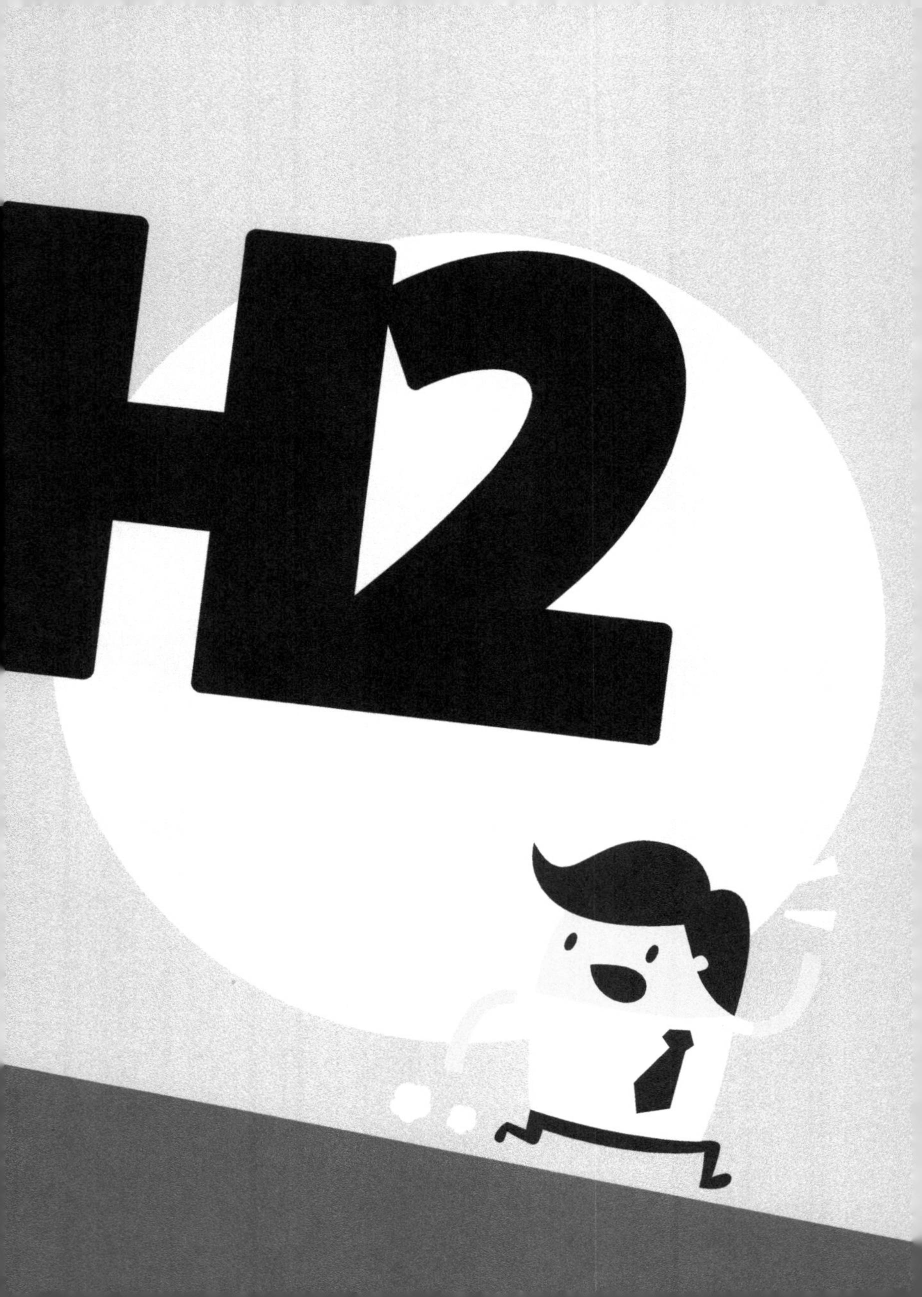
H2

Enclose Those Tags

Why wrap a field in HTML if that field doesn't contain a value? Remember **EnclosingTag**:

```
@Html.Sitecore().Field("myField", item, new { EnclosingTag = "h2" })
```

This wasn't supported in **Glass** so I added a pull request (don't say I never give you anything):

https://github.com/mikeedwards83/Glass.Mapper/pull/338

So you can use:

```
var someVar = new HtmlString(

    _glassHtml.Editable(item, i => i.myField, new { EnclosingTag = "h2"}

));
```

http://www.coretecdigital.com

Static vs Dynamic Binding

In the days of **reusability** there are fewer occasions where **static binding** will trump **dynamic binding**. While it does have its uses, a **static bind** should be a rare thing. Double check that you're using it correctly. Why output a hard coded rendering in your view? Think about the impact on testing/ personalization or reordering etc. For those who aren't clear:

Dynamic:

@Html.Sitecore().Placeholder("placeholder_name")

Static:

@Html.Sitecore().Controller(Controller, Action)

Always try to develop for flexibility; you can always opt for **placeholder settings** to control your **dynamic binding**.

Patch Me Up #2

It's that Pirate again! From **Volume 1**, remember?!

When **patching configs** we have two options, the **Patch namespace**, and the **Set namespace**. I only have a few sentences to tell you about them so please go and investigate for yourself and I'll show you a simple example, it's generally easier to use Set:

Patch:
```
<sites>
  <site name="helixbase">
    <patch:attribute name="targetHostName">demo.helixbase
    </patch:attribute>
  </site>
</sites>
```

Set:
```
<sites>
  <site name="helixbase" targetHostName="demo.helixbase">
  </site>
</sites>
```

The Nemesis To All Modules...

...is the **Anti package** (thankfully). I briefly mentioned this in **Volume 1** but let's talk a little more about creating an **anti package**. Before installing any **module** you should create an **Anti package** as you may decide in future that you do not want the **module** anymore. Without an **Anti package** you're on your own.

So open up **Sitecore rocks**, right-click your item in the **Sitecore Explorer** and use '*Tools->Create Package*', click '*Manage Packages*' in the *Package* tab, then select '*Anti Packages->Upload and Install*', finally select **Create Anti Package**... Or you could always use the anti package tool found in SPE. The **Anti package** is used to revert your files to the state they were in before Mr Marketplace Module joined the fun-bus.

Breaking Things

If you read the tip earlier you're using **buckets** if the tree has over **100 items**: gold stars for you!

Let's take this a step further... it's not all descendants that impact performance in our **> 100 items** tree, it's children. So if we're clever we may not need a bucket, we could instead break up these children into **sub folders**.

Won't somebody please, think of the children!

http://www.coretecdigital.com

Hidden Components

So you're a **personalization** extraordinaire and you've implemented it everywhere. However, for one of your components you've added a rule to *Hide the component*. Off you go to the **Experience Editor** and you can't see the component anymore! Oh no! Don't fear, one option to bring it back is *Presentation details->rendering->personalize*

Use it if your rendering was **hidden** by a personalization rule.

#Hashtags

You thought **hashtags** were for social media?! Nope, try one

in your Sitecore queries to escape text:

query:/sitecore/content/home/#about me#/*

http://www.coretecdigital.com

Keep Views Dumb

Do you use helpers in your views, or even business logic?! Why not keep your views as dumb as possible instead? On page 79 we mentioned **EnclosingTags**. Expanding on this I want to drum home the point about keeping **views dumb**.

Use the **Glass Html** object to pass in **Html Strings** rather than add complexity to a view. It's not only **EnclosingTags** that we can use as a parameter:

http://bit.ly/2ltKkXh

The **Glass Html** object – a great way to keep your views clean. If you're not using **Glass**, pass something like the following to your view:

viewModel.someProperty = FieldRender.Render(item, "FieldValue"));

Keeping In Sync

Looking to setup an **async task** in the controller rendering? Don't: it's not supported.

You could use an **async MVC controller** with a custom route but if you're trying to work **asynchronously** with your controller rendering, you could be in for a headache!

http://www.coretecdigital.com

Dictionary Fun

So you have a **validation message** which you get from a lovely Sitecore dictionary, great for localization... But remember, you can use *{0}* in dictionary items, then use *string.Format* in source.

You may want to display *"Field restricted to x characters"* for example.

{0} - Great for **validation** huh? There's a hero in this zero.

Forced Comments, Awkward!

Sometimes it's a **workflow** annoyance to force a **comment** on absolutely everything. Don't fret: Sitecore has the answer.

On your workflow **publish command** use 'suppress comment' to remove the need for a comment.

The Power Of The Search Tool

When you're navigating the **Content Editor**, the search tool is extremely powerful. Select your item and then click on the **Search icon** next to the 'Content' tab, or right-click your item and select 'Search'. You can perform many tasks such as filtering child items by *'template/author/edited by'*, or checking the creation date of a rendering and so on. The **search tool** is overlooked for some reason but it's your ticket to finding a lot of information, and who doesn't like information?!... Be careful with it though, knowledge is power!

Querying Things

Why not use a **Sitecore query** in your glass fluent mappings? Plus, you also know what the hashtag does now, so you're a query supremo:

.Query($".//[@@templateid='{Templates.SomeItem.TemplateId.ToString("B").ToUpper()}']")*

Check out a live example in **Helix Base**:

http://bit.ly/2Icu8XO

#ShamelessPlug

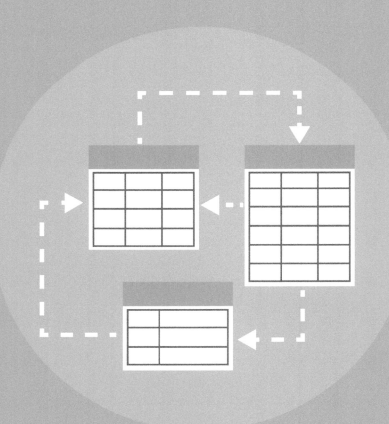

Link Management Fun

Open up your *ShowConfig.aspx* tool and search for the following:

<linkManager defaultProvider="sitecore">

Look at all those juicy link options! Want to embed the language in your url? No problem! Want to use item display names? No problem! Take a look at the options and configure accordingly.

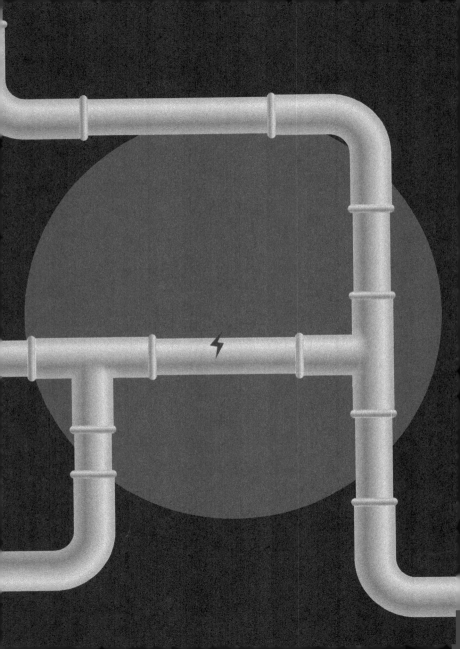

Crack Open The Pipe

So you have a rendering with a **Datasource Location** assigned, you're doing well, but what if you want to use more than one **Datasource Location**? Or you have a multi site setup so you want to use a **query** in this field? It's as easy as adding a **pipe**:

SomeDatasourceLocation | AnotherDataSourceLocation

I hope that **pipe** is big enough for you to take note, **pipe** your **Datasource Locations** FTW :partyparrot:

Composition vs Inheritance

Some genius added **composition** to Glass fluent config:

http://bit.ly/2Cf9wLL

I like that guy! I personally prefer **composition** over the hierarchy of **inheritance**, there's nothing worse than *CTRL+clicking* your way through a nested bunch of implemented interfaces. The Inheritance hierarchy can become complex, so have a little think about using **composition**. Something you should at least be aware of.

Unicorn Sync Fails

From time to time there are ***Unicorn sync issues/warnings*** after a dev checks in changes. Save the time spent fixing these by always observing the following step:

If you ever make a change to an item that's **serialized** in **Unicorn**, always press the 'serialize item' button on the developer toolbar. Just press it anyway, even if you think your changes won't cause any sync issues.

Impossible

Changing Things

Did you add the wrong template to an item, or perhaps you fancy changing it? Don't go deleting it and starting again, simply select **Configure->Change** under 'Template' in your ribbon.

This relates to the tip on page 5. If you refactor template fields you can lose data, unless you decide to do this... when splitting a template into base templates simply drag and drop your fields from the origin to a new template. Job done!

Which Idiot Wrote This Code?!

…probably some 'idiot' who had thought about something you hadn't.

You never know what conditions the previous dev was working under, or if they were thinking about something you hadn't. Not everything is **black and white** in this industry so always think carefully about your changes, and about the changes of your predecessors.

This applies to your Sitecore codebase and any other codebase you ever have, or ever will, work on.

Highlighting Things

We often wait around for Sitecore to recycle, give yourself a visual indicator by **selecting all** text on the page. You'll know when that page has refreshed because you'll see your highlight disappear. On a dual monitor setup this could be out the corner of your eye! Try it.

Exclude Files

Did you know you can **exclude files** from deployment? Open your publish profile *.pubxml* and add the following for example just before </PropertyGroup> :

<ExcludeFilesFromDeployment>bin\Sitecore.Kernel.dll;bin\Sitecore.Mvc.dll;bin\Sitecore.Mvc.Analytics.dll;Web.config</ExcludeFilesFromDeployment>

You can also use the 'PublishIgnore' NuGet package to exclude Sitecore dlls:

https://www.nuget.org/packages/PublishIgnore/

Neat!

Auto Sync'age

We started **Volume 1** with a content publish tip (you'll remember because you read it, right?!). Earlier on I also mentioned that we'd talk more about the Sitecore rocks **auto publish** feature so here we go...

Sitecore rocks contains a **folder sync** option that will auto push content to your webroot. Great for any files that don't recycle the application pool (razor views, css etc). With your Visual Studio project connected to your Sitecore instance right-click on your desired folder and select **Sitecore->Start Folder Sync.** Then select your **target folder** and a **sync mode** and you're away! Any changes to the content in this folder will be auto pushed to your target in the webroot. Gotta love Sitecore rocks! :heart:

Solr Cores

Create **separate cores** for your requirements e.g. are you working on a **news index** listing? Then setup a 'news' core.

Also go and read about **stored=true** and **indexed=false** to decide which fields should be stored in your index (for performance reasons).

While we're doing well, why not use a naming convention so that your cores have a different name on disk? In each of your configs setup something like...

```
<param desc="name">$(id)</param>
<param desc="core">SomeNAME _$(id)</param>
```

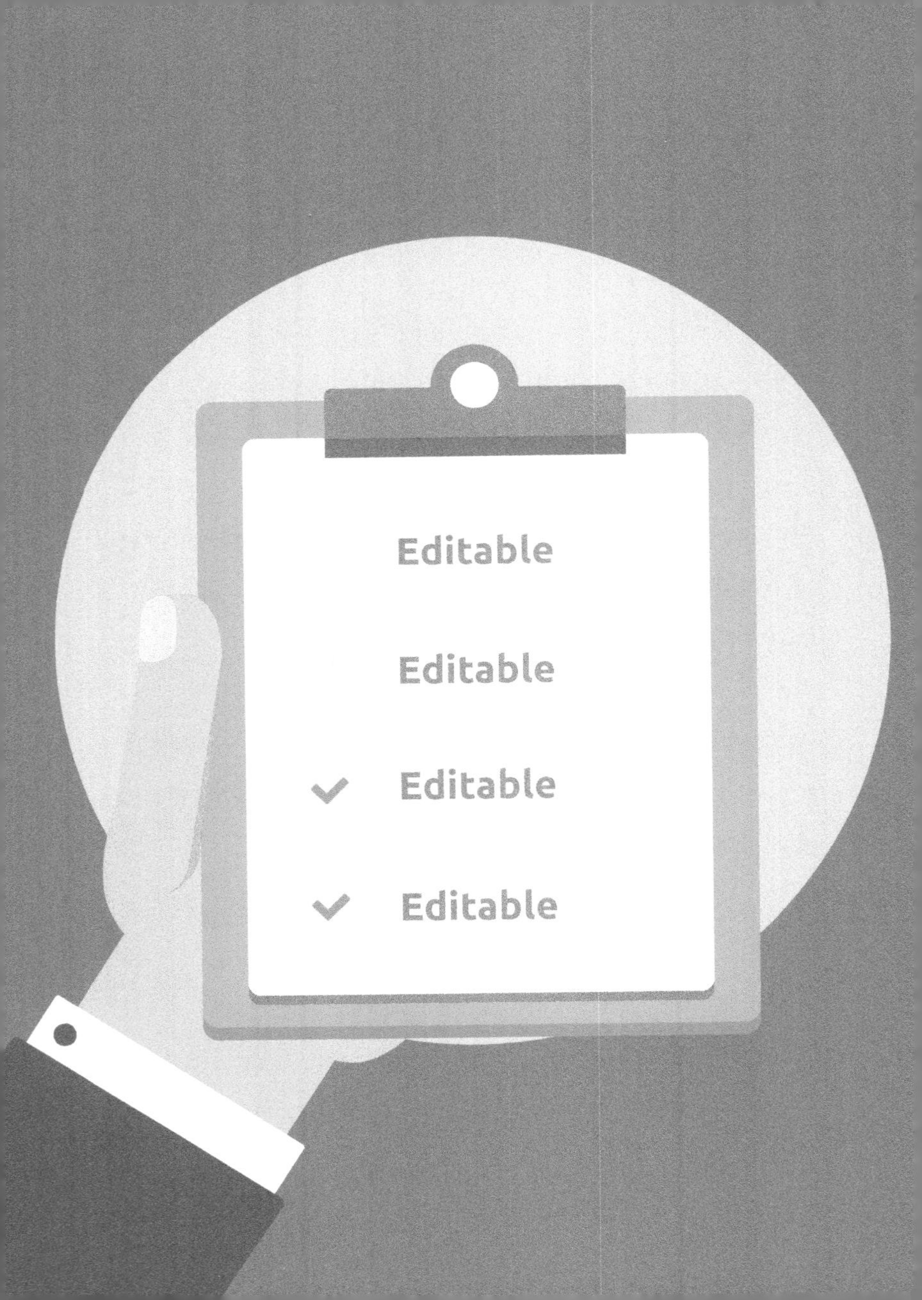
Editable
Editable
Editable
Editable

Editable Placeholders

Referring to **Volume 1** yet again, I told you that your editors are naughty, so why are your **placeholders** editable?

Go through them all now and uncheck 'editable' or your content team will wreak havoc!

Server Gatekeepers

So some crazy server admin is stuck in the comfort zone and won't give you access to the servers? Fortunately if you're an admin in Sitecore you can still view the logs:

Desktop -> Reporting Tools -> Log Viewer

Chew on that one Mr Server admin!

http://www.coretecdigital.com

Insert Option All The Things

When it comes to adding page content... regular users cannot use *'insert from template'*, that would create a mess. So here's another tip that's geared towards thinking about your authors:

Make sure you assign **insert options** to EVERYTHING!

...Insert option all the things!

Stay On Piste

Similar to the .NET superstar tip in **Volume 1**, make sure you stay on the **Sitecore piste**. Often problems that can be easily handled natively in Sitecore are tackled with complex solutions that introduce instability. So spend time learning about native Sitecore features (books help!) and stay on the **Sitecore piste** - Do not add processors to pipelines unless it's an absolute requirement.

The native option might not be as 'feature rich' as your bespoke solution but it usually brings benefits that top whatever complexity you're introducing into your Sitecore instance. Always opt for **efficiency** over complexity. Keep it **Sitecorey** you're a **Sitecorian** now, **Sitecore-ify** your solutions, do not introduce over engineered instability, do not turn Sitecore into your own separate MVC application. Lesson over!